YOU CAN'T BE

TOO CAREFUL

ILLUSTRATIONS BY

YOU CAN'T BE

CAUTIONARY TALES BY

WORKMAN PUBLISHING

PIERRE LE-TAN

TOO CAREFUL

DAVID PRYCE-JONES

NEW YORK

Library of Congress Cataloging-in-Publi-
cation Data: Pryce-Jones, David, 1936–You
can't be too careful: cautionary tales / by
David Pryce-Jones; illustrations by Pierre Le-
Tan. p. cm. ISBN 1-56305-156-7 1.
American wit and humor. I. Le-Tan, Pierre.
II. Title. PN6162.P78 1992 081'.0207—
dc20. Workman books are available at special
discounts when purchased in bulk for
premiums and sales promotions as well as for
fund-raising or educational use. Special
editions or book excerpts can also be created
to specification. For details, contact the
Special Sales Director at the address below.
Workman Publishing Company, Inc., 708
Broadway, New York, NY 10003. Manu-
factured in the United States of America.
First printing October 1992 10 9 8 7 6 5 4
3 2 1 Design by Louise Fili & Lee Bearson.

CONTENTS

※

"You can't be too careful." This is an indispensable maxim for guidance in a universe like ours, reputedly the product of the Big Bang. What else is daily life but a series of accidents, one of which ultimately must settle the score of every mother's child? Is experience anything except a process of learning to recognize the potential in everything for accident and then prudently to get out of the way?

Everything that happens to us mixes the comic and the tragic in unforeseen ways, and each of us must decide where the balance is to lie. Death itself, in this view, is only another happening, so that what is fatal also can have its humor: a killing joke, you might say.

In the midst of life we are in death. Each one of the unfortunate victims described here got up that last morning without the least intimation that the hourglass was down to a few vanishing grains of sand. For years now I have been clipping from newspapers accounts of untimely deaths. All those collected here are therefore a matter of public record, though out of the enormity of it I have replaced names with initials. As a rule newspapers print these accounts on an inside page, in a rather summary fashion, as though to acknowledge the bewilderment that anyone could have died in such an unlikely manner.

Go to war, wrestle with a crocodile, or rob a bank, and you can be sure that you are in greater danger than if you stay at home to watch television (although even that can be fatal, as some people in Bodrum were unlucky enough to learn). Here are victims who were going about their business as we all do. They could not have imagined the malevolence of familiar objects, or the end of what must have seemed a normal pastime or pursuit. Some of them were having fun, making friends or even love, and they were displaying high spirits, or joking. Some happened to be wearing something that proved unsuitable. Electric guitars, footstools, chewing gum, toothpicks, goldfish, a tennis ball—all contained lethal qualities never suspected. Other victims stumbled and slipped; they may have done nothing except stand and stare. Perhaps strangest of all, things fell out of the skies above. Aeschylus, the great dramatist of classical Greece, is supposed to have been killed by a tortoise falling on his bald pate, but here we have poor Ghulam of Srinagar, down whose neck a hawk dropped a viper. People happened to be in the wrong place at the wrong time, and there was absolutely nothing to be done about it. One way or another, the universe has snatched them into its unfathomable workings, and that's that.

"The human comedy" is an idea that goes back a

long way because it expresses one of the most profound of responses. What can't be cured must be endured. How are we otherwise to come to terms with the state of shock induced by accident? So interwoven are tragedy and comedy that death itself—the supreme accident—is as fit a subject for laughter as it is for tears. The dimension of death is what makes life wonderful and terrifying at the same time. Each of these accidental deaths reveals an imaginative truth about human existence that is found only in the work of the greatest novelists.

❉

Among those to be thanked for contributions to this gathering on the Elysian fields are Clarissa Pryce-Jones, Adam Pryce-Jones, Jack Diggle, Candida Mostyn-Owen, Jessica Shukman, and Marilyn and Hugh Nissenson.

LOVE & OTHER VANITIES

The plumber of Salonika

A plumber died after jumping naked from his girlfriend's third-floor apartment near Salonika, Greece, to escape from the enraged husband who caught them in bed.

❊

The naked truth was too much for a Frankfurt pensioner of seventy-seven who hired a striptease dancer to perform in his flat. Police said he died of a heart attack during the routine.

❊

A man reclining with a woman on top of a piano at a topless nightclub in San Francisco was crushed to death when the piano was raised to the ceiling as part of the show. The woman escaped through a ceiling hatch.

❊

A woman was rescued after being trapped in a car, under the dead body of her naked lover, for four days. Alerted by screams coming from the garage of an abandoned house, firemen found Daisy G. of West Akron, Ohio, wedged under the 210-pound body of James D. She told police they were having sex when he died.

❋

A couple's lovemaking on top of a 220-foot cliff ended in death for one of them, an inquest at Newport, Isle of Wight, was told. They were kissing, cuddling, and rolling about when Mr. Michael R. rolled over the cliff edge. "Michael was alongside me, and in due course, on top of me," Mrs. C. said. "We had not had sex, but we were contemplating it. About that time he appeared to slip away from me. He did not make any sound at all. I think he may have rolled over a couple of times. I grasped hold of the grass to stop myself from slipping over. I managed to look over the cliff and saw he had gone down feet first with his arms in the air, and then out of sight."

✳

A thirty-four-year-old man died of blood poisoning in Varna, Bulgaria, after his wife, who had eaten contaminated fish, playfully bit the lobe of his ear.

✳

Miss Eleanor B., a seventy-year-old actress, was smothered to death by a collection of personal newspaper clippings that fell on her while she was alone in her New York apartment.

✳

An Iranian man killed himself after finding his bride suffocated in a suitcase during an attempt to smuggle her into the United States. The body of the woman was found in a large suitcase revolving around a luggage carousel at Los Angeles International Airport.

❉

A Frenchwoman has been sentenced to five years in jail for killing her husband by regularly feeding him fruit tart laced with a powerful tranquilizer. Mme Marcelle de S. told a court in Metz that she had not meant to kill her husband with the sedatives, but just to keep him quiet. She would arrange the fruit in such a way that she knew which piece to give him.

In Perryville, Missouri, a woman fired a gun at two former classmates as they exchanged wedding vows and then killed herself with a shot to the head. The woman, Sherry Ann K., knew the couple only slightly, but a yearbook photograph of the groom was found in her wallet. "The way the groom described it, it was a crush," said a member of the family. The wedding later resumed, but at the reception the bride's grandmother suffered a fatal heart attack.

❋

Encarnacion G. died after a baker gave her a huge quantity of salt to eat and then beat her. He was trying to exorcise the devil, hospital sources in Granada said.

❋

Mr. Alan N., the pioneer of spiritual medicine from St. Austell, died after tripping over his healing stool.

※

At least twenty-six people, most of them middle-aged women, plunged to their deaths in East Java in a scramble to reach a waterfall they believed had the power to restore youth.

※

Richard B., who attended a chapel in Cartersville, Georgia, where members handle poisonous snakes as a test of faith to see if God wants them to live or die, was bitten by a rattlesnake and died.

※

A woman whose hair burst into flames when she lit a cigarette after spraying herself with perfume died from burns. Mrs. Sheila R., the wife of a financial consultant, was found in the back garden of her house in Preston with flames coming from the top of her head. She told a neighbor that it happened when she lit the cigarette after using the perfume. Mr. Christopher Foulweather, forensic expert, said he examined two sprays, Just Musk by Lentheric and Charlie by Revlon, and both had contents comparable with methylated spirits.

A fifteen-year-old girl died from blood poisoning a month after having an ear pierced at a High Wycombe jewelry shop.

FREE FALL

A bucket of tar

A thirty-two-year-old woman died when a bucket of tar fell fifty feet from a scaffolding and hit her on the head.

＊

Two men were killed when a ship's crane swung out of control and dropped a car on them as it was being unloaded at Tilbury Docks, Essex.

＊

A partly built block of apartment buildings collapsed in Cocoa Beach, Florida, killing at least four workers, when a crane dropped a bucket of concrete through the freshly poured roof.

＊

A jobless seventeen-year-old who found he could get free drinks from vending machines by rocking them died after an eight-hundred-pound machine fell on top of him, an inquest at St. Pancras heard.

✻

A sixty-one-year-old woman died after accidentally being hit on the head by a baton at a majorette display in Weston-super-Mare, Avon.

✻

A twenty-eight-year-old Brooklyn woman was killed when she was struck on the head by a flowerpot that had been knocked off an eighth-floor ledge, apparently by a bolt of lightning.

Stephen McD. of Woking, Surrey, was killed on Curzon Street, London, when a plate-glass window, dislodged by high winds, fell forty-five feet and hit him on the head.

❋

A woman witch doctor was killed and four men injured when the bus stop shelter in which they were sleeping was demolished. Workmen, unaware of the group, wrapped chains around the shelter and used a truck to pull it down.

❋

Nine people died in Ho Chi Minh City after a bridge collapsed under the weight of a fifty-strong crowd that had gathered to watch a girl commit suicide. The girl was rescued.

❋

A twenty-five-year-old Frenchwoman
who jumped 150 feet to her death
from a spiral staircase in one of
Notre-Dame Cathedral's twin towers
also killed a Canadian woman tourist standing
on the pavement below.

✸

Lightning struck a cemetery bell tower in Urbana,
Illinois, toppling part of the structure onto a homeless
man who was sleeping inside.

✸

Mr. Henry S. slipped to his death on the stairs of his
home in Brixton because he was wearing shiny silk socks,
a Southwark inquest was told.

A man drowned after jumping from a bridge into the River Exe at Tiverton, Devon, to retrieve his shoe.

❈

Mr. David G. of Bristol broke his neck when he dived twenty-five feet from Torquay Pier into eighteen inches of water. He failed to notice that the tide had gone out.

❈

A senior RAF officer, Wing Commander Graham G., lost his balance while sliding down a banister for a prank at the War Office in Whitehall and plunged eighty feet to his death. Wing Commander Peter S. said the accident happened after his colleague had chaired a difficult meeting that had gone on for several hours.

"Afterwards, when we got into the lift," said the

wing commander, "others were debating whether to take the lift or walk. Graham called to them: 'Take the lift, the stairs, or slide down the banister.' He sat on the banister sidesaddle, then suddenly fell back into the stairwell."

❈

Two lawyers tried to settle "a friendly argument" about the Olympics by racing down a hallway at their law firm. One who had poor eyesight crashed through a thirty-ninth-floor window and plunged to his death.

❈

An Englishman identified by French police as Mr. Peter E. of St. Mary's, Cambridge, was killed when he fell fifteen feet from a parapet at Lyons. He was sunbathing and fell when he dozed off.

Mr. Frank W. died after a "tightrope walk" along a highway overpass went wrong. Police said that Mr. W. had been "showing off" to four friends after a night out. He lost his balance and fell twenty feet while trying to tiptoe along a three-inch ledge on railings over the highway at Warmsworth, near Doncaster.

❈

A workman fell 250 feet to his death on a beach at La Coupée, Sark, in the Channel Islands, while attempting to do handstands on some railings.

❈

Mr. Peter F. died after a fall from the 451-foot summit of the Great Pyramid at Giza. He had climbed the pyramid illegally and had gone to sleep at the top.

A U.S. Navy sailor was killed and another seriously injured when they fell into the crater of Mount Vesuvius. Police said the two went to the edge for a better view and lost their balance, plunging three hundred feet.

✵

Mr. Stephen W. saw his wife, L., plunge 150 feet to her death from the cliff top at Flamborough Head. She overreached when trying to retrieve a kite.

✵

A woman died when she fell five feet down a hole that suddenly opened in her garden as she was taking in the washing. The hole at the house, near St. Austell, might have been an old well or exploratory mine shaft.

An escapologist fell sixty feet to his death during his first public performance of a new stunt. Mr. Trevor R. was supposed to escape from a straitjacket while suspended by a paraffin-dipped burning rope. But the rope burned through because he didn't realize that he had to soak it in water to repel the paraffin.

A dairy deliveryman, Joseph L., was fatally injured when a five-hundred-pound rack of Nutty Buddies fell on him at a supermarket in Tampa, Florida. He had rolled the ice cream onto a hydraulic lift at the rear of his truck. Normally, an eight-inch rim that sticks up from the lift keeps the rack in place. However, the rim was not up and the rack rolled over on top of him.

HEALTH &
EFFICIENCY

Fishing for carp

An Ivory Coast girl choked to death when she accidentally swallowed a live carp while fishing.

A forty-nine-year-old woman died after swallowing a silver-plated teaspoon, a Croydon inquest was told. It was not known when Miss Doris H. swallowed the spoon, first seen on an X-ray last year. Mr. David H., pathologist, said he thought the spoon, which bore the marking of the old London County Council, had been in her stomach for a considerable time. Miss H. died from metal poisoning.

A twenty-eight-year-old man died when a toothpick he had swallowed six months before pierced a main artery.

Mr. Llewellyn N. choked to death when he tried to swallow a pickled onion whole during tea.

✻

An Irish poet, John J., choked to death on a ham roll while attending a conference at the Park Hotel in Cardiff.

✻

Melissa S. died after suffocating on a tiny sliver of peach she was eating in the early morning at her home.

✻

A piece of chewing gum killed Miss Gillian B., a Westminster inquest was told. Miss B. collapsed in the street while talking. Although the chewing gum was removed from her windpipe the next day, she died two months later.

Robert G. choked to death in a pub in Cupar, Fife, after he put a billiard ball in his mouth for a joke.

✵

A seven-year-old boy died when he was ejected through the canopy of a Navy jet. The plane was on display in a Fourth of July show for an estimated 100,000 visitors at Willow Grove Naval Air Station in Pennsylvania.

A U.S. Navy spokesman said it was not known how John P. managed to trigger the ejection device. Ten spectators at the stairway to the cockpit of the S-3 Viking jet were also injured by the cannonlike explosion that hurled the pilot's seat and the boy more than fifty feet into the air.

✵

A soldier, age twenty-two, drowned in the sea off Bangor Pier, Ulster. Police believed he had gone to the edge of the pier to relieve himself and had slipped into the sea.

❋

A heavy drinker who decided to cut down his intake died from a heart attack caused by alcohol withdrawal, an inquest at Preston, Lancashire, was told.

❋

The bartender who refereed a gin-drinking contest in which two drinkers died later died of a heart attack himself. His widow said he died of grief after hearing that he might be prosecuted for manslaughter for officiating at the contest.

❋

A young woman drank herself to death in Miami—with water. She had been drinking four gallons a day in an attempt to cleanse her body of falsely suspected cancer. Dr. Ronald W., Dade County deputy medical examiner, said Miss C. destroyed her body's chemical balance with excessive water drinking.

※

A man suffering from ringing in the ears, who took drugs and alcohol to get relief, died when he fell asleep in an awkward position in front of the fire. Professor David B., pathologist, said the awkward position cut off oxygen to his limbs, which caused kidney failure.

The Hammersmith coroner said: "This usually happens when people are lying in bombed-out buildings in wartime."

A Thai building worker who ate four bags of locusts as a snack died of insecticide poisoning.

✻

A rat catcher who called at a school was told by a cook to remove some poisoned bait that he had put on a kitchen table because she thought it was not safe near food.

He replied that there was no danger, then ate some of the bait. He was admitted to the hospital writhing in pain and died a month later.

✻

A sixty-year-old machinist decided to give a new toilet cleaner a good start by getting the factory toilets spotless for his arrival. But an inquest at Sheffield was told that Mr. Bob M. mixed two cleaning fluids, and together they gave off chlorine gas. Mr. M. inhaled the fumes and died of heart failure.

A six-foot four-inch former diplomat died of brain hemorrhage after repeatedly hitting his head on low door frames and cupboards. His wife, Mrs. Sophia K., told the inquest: "Because my husband was so tall he had a tendency of banging his head."

NOAH'S ARK

Janco and his pythons

Two 12-foot pythons crushed Janco S., their trainer, to death before hundreds of spectators at a Naples circus.

※

A polar bear killed an Austrian tourist in Spitsbergen, the Norwegian Arctic Ocean territory. The thirty-three-year-old tourist was camping with friends near Magalena Fjord when he heard scratching on his tent. He went out to investigate and was knocked down and killed by the bear, which swam off with his body.

※

Two circus elephants broke out of their ring in Salerno, Italy, and trampled to death a thirty-five-year-old woman walking on a nearby street. The elephants were later caught and taken back to the circus.

A nurse was bending over a prostrate antelope, preparing to administer a sedative, when the animal suddenly raised its head and pierced the nurse's throat with a horn.

✵

A Japanese prawn diver died when a needlefish, attracted by the light he was carrying, stabbed him in the neck.

✵

A fisherman, Mr. Anthony F., died after being impaled by a fork-tail alligator garfish that leapt out of the sea off Sri Lanka.

✵

Two youths were killed when an Indian antelope jumped onto their car, causing it to crash. The animal, a nilgai, leapt ten feet, crashed through the car's windshield, and tore the roof off in the accident on a country lane in Petham, Kent.

Seven farm workers were asphyxiated one by one in a manure pit at a pig farm in the village of Ukrainskaya, three hundred miles south of Moscow. Each man had gone in to try to rescue the others.

Mr. Yannis D., a hundred-year-old Greek farmer, was killed by an amorous ram that gored him in the stomach when he tried to stop it from mating with one of his goats.

A wild elephant, believed to be in heat, crushed to death a Buddhist monk and a businessman trying to photograph it, Thai authorities reported.

❅

Antonio B., who killed more than two thousand bulls in a thirty-year career as a leading matador, died in Madrid from injuries received when a yearling cow charged him from behind at a ranch.

❅

A hermit who claimed he could hypnotize and tame a marauding jaguar lost his wager with villagers near Caracas, Venezuela. The jaguar savaged him to death.

A twenty-eight-year-old man suffocated in his living room, a Leeds inquest was told. The coroner, Mr. James W., was told that the gas flue at the house was blocked with debris and a bird flew out when the gas fire was removed.

❉

A spider in a gas burner led to a man's death. Mr. Terence L., a gas technician, said a large household spider got into a sink water unit and restricted the air intake, producing a flame with an extremely high carbon monoxide context. Professor James C., pathologist, told the St. Pancras coroner that Mr. William N. died from carbon monoxide poisoning at his home.

❉

A seven-month-old girl was slowly squeezed to death by the family pet—a seven-foot ten-inch python—as her parents slept in the adjoining room of their Dallas home.

The snake, which had escaped from a terrarium in the living room, bit the child repeatedly, then coiled around her body, squeezing her to death. Mr. and Mrs. Bob D. found their daughter dead in her crib when they rose shortly before 8:00 A.M. The snake had crawled up to a shelf and was resting there placidly.

To save the life of her goldfish, a woman drowned in her ornamental pond. Mrs. Elizabeth B., of Radlett Park, was attempting to melt ice with hot water when she fell through into the freezing water. Mr. Philip B., her husband, said a recent radio program had advised people concerned about their fish to melt ice on their ponds rather than break it.

❋

A truck driver who tried to rescue a neighbor's kitten when his dog chased it up a tree died after he fell head-first from the tall poplar. Mr. Michael C. had reached the kitten and tucked it into his anorak when he fell. The kitten survived. Its owner, Mrs. Sylvia A., said Mr. C.'s wife had advised him to leave the animal in the tree, "but he was determined to get it down."

❋

A man fell to his death from the twenty-second floor of a high-rise in Hammersmith while trying to rescue his kitten. Mr. George H. became trapped in a window and fell two hundred feet after dangling by his hands. The kitten survived.

✻

Hundreds of monkeys bit and scratched a boy of nine to death in a Borneo animal reserve after he and three other boys refused to give up their lunch boxes. His companions escaped unharmed when a passing farmer diverted the monkeys with a bunch of bananas.

✻

A viper dropped from the claws of a hawk overhead as Ghulam N. was fixing his motorscooter on the road from Srinagar to his home fifteen miles away. The viper, falling on Ghulam N., bit his neck, and he died within minutes. The hawk retrieved the snake and flew off.

✻

A dog accidentally pulled the trigger of a shotgun with its legs, killing Yukiyasu Y., the son of its owner, while all three were traveling in a car, police said.

✻

A dog that fell from a thirteenth-floor balcony in Buenos Aires triggered three deaths in a row. It landed on a seventy-five-year-old woman, killing her instantly. Another woman in a crowd that gathered at the scene was knocked down by a bus, and a man who saw both incidents suffered a heart attack and died.

✻

WORK & PLAY

A strong mistral wind

In spite of the strong mistral wind, many bathers were still on the beach in the Riviera when a violent gust of wind lifted an umbrella from its fixing in the sand, sending it flying several meters. The umbrella's point entered one woman's chest and pierced her heart.

※

Nine people were killed when a television set exploded, starting a fire and natural gas blast that destroyed a house in Bodrum, Turkey.

※

A girl dancing barefoot at a riverside barbecue party to celebrate the Conservatives' General Election victory died after touching faulty electrical disco lighting. An Electricity Board engineer said the wiring had a number of defects and anyone in bare feet could have received an electrical shock.

※

A municipal worker sent to cut off power at a house in Gweru clipped the wrong wire, making the water pipes live. The occupant, who had defaulted on his payments, took a shower and was killed.

※

Murderer Michael G., who escaped the electric chair after an appeal, was electrocuted accidentally while sitting on a steel toilet in his cell in Columbia, South Carolina.

He was trying to repair earphones connected to his television set when he bit into a live wire.

※

Thirty-five passengers were electrocuted when an over-crowded inter-city bus carrying old bicycles on its roof came in contact with roadside electricity wires, the Uttar Pradesh state police said.

❈

A man was electrocuted in his back garden while fitting a water pump in a fish pond. The shock killed Michael N. when he put his hand in the water to find out why the pump would not work.

❈

Marc B. attached a wire to his arm so an automatically triggered 220-volt electrical charge would wake him in the morning. But instead it killed him, police in Chartres, France, said.

Officials of the Hyōgo Prefecture Labor Standards Bureau announced that the arm of a robot processing gears for cars had beaten to death a factory worker after stabbing him in the back. Kenju U., a robot repair worker, was apparently working on the robot when he accidentally brushed the machine's "on-off" switch. Mr. U. was pinned against the gear-manufacturing unit and repeatedly struck by the robot.

❋

Botanist Lyle W. was the first American scientist to study the inexorable Asian water plant hydrilla, which kills fish by the millions in waters choked by its amazingly rapid growth—up to an inch per day. Dr. W., conducting underwater research on the weed, became entangled in its stringy vines and drowned.

Mr. Michael M., lead guitarist in a four-man rhythm group, died after suffering two shocks from his electric guitar before an audience of 250 during a Saturday night concert at a workingmen's club.

＊

A sixty-two-year-old Pentecostal preacher was electrocuted in Stockholm in front of a congregation of two hundred as he was about to baptize a boy.

Pentecostal baptism is by total immersion, and fonts in Sweden are heated electrically. The preacher, who was standing in water up to his waist, collapsed when an assistant handed him a microphone.

＊

The Reverend James G., a Baptist minister, drowned as he prepared to baptize four new members of the church in the Silver Park River, Transvaal.

Mr. G. stepped into the water, praying: "Lord, I am coming to baptize these people in the name of the Father, the Son, and the Holy Spirit." As he said the words "Holy Spirit," he sank into the mud. A fellow minister, the Reverend Nelson M., dived twice into the river in a vain rescue attempt.

※

Raymond P. of Melbourne tried the snooker shot of a lifetime—suspended upside down over the table, hanging by his legs from the rafters. But he slipped, crashed headfirst on the concrete floor, and died.

※

A flash flood swept at least ten secondary-school students to their deaths when workers unaware of the students opened the gates of a reservoir.

Rescue officials said four hundred students from three Taipei schools were having an end-of-term picnic in the dry river bed below the reservoir when the flood occurred.

※

A Japanese worker was killed by an electrical shock while helping to remove 1,340 huge blue parasols placed in a Japanese valley by the artist Christo. It was the second death to hit Christo's $8.5 million, two-nation umbrella art project. High winds blew one of the 448-pound umbrellas across a road at the project's California site, crushing a woman against a boulder.

Martin S., of Merseyside, died after he was hit in the chest by a golf ball at Formby Golf Club, near Southport.

※

One man was killed and eight others injured when the branch of a tree from which they were watching an international cricket match at Gujranwala, Pakistan, broke under their weight.

※

A man fell to his death while playing football with his workmates on the second story of a disused warehouse at a cheese factory in North Tawton, Devon.

※

Richard W., a tennis linesman,
of Lexington, Massachusetts,
died of injuries he suffered
when he was hit by a ball
and fell backward on
his head during the
U.S. Open.

❊

A county hockey player died when he fell on his stick as he played in a league game. Malcolm H. was dribbling the ball when his stick jammed into the ground and he ran into it at full speed. The stick rammed him in the chest.

❊

A schoolboy on a weekend fishing trip was killed when a four-ounce lead weight cast by another angler at South Shields, Tyneside, struck him on the head.

❀

An angler died after struggling to land a sixteen-pound salmon. Mr. Frederick W., a retired research chemist, collapsed and died on the banks of the River Wye near Hereford after landing a fish. His son Christopher said: "I think the excitement must have been too much for him. We are probably going to eat the fish. I think he would have approved."

❀

A young American skier wearing nylon trousers slid 150 yards to his death in New Zealand's Southern Alps after he sat down to rest, a park ranger said, adding, "He had no way of stopping himself."

✹

A chemistry teacher was killed when he fell off a bicycle he had built from spare parts but which could not go around corners. Mr. George P. died after being thrown over the handlebars the first time he rode the bicycle. A policeman said: "If the handlebars were turned slightly to the right, then the left pedal jammed the front wheel, causing the cycle to stop abruptly."

✹

A businessman was killed when lightning struck the metal zipper on his trousers while he was playing golf in Kyoto, Japan.

Police are investigating the death of Mr. Brian B., a forty-one-year-old man who is thought to have blown himself up while making a device to scare away rooks from his garden.

❋

A forty-six-year-old baseball umpire was killed in Tokyo when lightning struck a metal badge on his cap during a children's match.

❋

The metal in a woman's bra probably attracted the lightning that caused her death as she walked through a park in a severe storm. Mrs. Iris S. was found lying under a

tree in Queen's Park, Willesden. Dr. Iain W., a pathologist, said a burn mark on the chest appeared to match
exactly the reinforced area of Mrs. S.'s bra.

❈

Lawyer N. Graves T. stood up in a boat on a lake during a
thunderstorm, raised his hands to the heavens, and
shouted: "Here I am!" Seconds later, a bolt of lightning
struck him dead. Mr. T. had been defending a man accused
of recklessness in a boating accident that had killed three
people on the same lake in Shreveport, Louisiana.

❈

A woman was killed when her sari became entangled in
the axle of a miniature train at the Drayton Manor Park
and Zoo near Tamworth, Staffordshire.

A ten-pence coin cost Mr. Jim H., an amusement park worker of Reading, Berkshire, his life when he bent down to pick up the money and was hit on the head by a Dive Bomber, one of the amusements at a fairground in Maidenhead.

❈

Seven people died in the northern Portuguese town of Vila Real after lightning set their house on fire, brought down a nearby power pylon, and electrified the ground outside.

❈

Dr. Ole B., a Dane, died when a fit of laughter at the John Cleese film *A Fish Called Wanda* brought on a heart attack at a cinema.

Richard P., a student, was killed in a fall from a freight train in central France, police said.

P. had been celebrating his birthday with four friends and all had been drinking heavily. As a joke, the friends put P., asleep, on a freight car, but the train started suddenly. P. woke up, apparently fell between the cars, and was crushed under the train.

❉

A schoolboy died after shaking his head violently in time to the music at a hard rock concert. Christopher T. was "head-banging" at a concert by the Yorkshire-based Saxon group in Wolverhampton's civic hall. "The exaggerated head movements at the concert were the primary cause of his death," Dr. Shirley W., pathologist, told the inquest at Wolverhampton.

THE WAGES OF CRIME

the getaway

A fifty-six-year-old thief in Alicante died after choking on his false teeth while fleeing from a woman he had just robbed.

✻

Burglar Camelo N. died after breaking into a villa and raiding the fridge, which contained poisoned food. His partner, Armando D., had to give himself up as he called an ambulance. The food had been prepared by the owner to rid his garden shed in Enna, Sicily, of rats.

✻

A youth caught stealing bed quilts from a Birmingham store climbed a drainpipe to escape a store detectives but fell to his death when the pipe broke away from the wall.

✻

Many old houses have chimneys running through their interiors, and many burglars have risked their lives getting in that way. Workmen called into a Bradford

office complex to inspect the central heating found a decomposed body in the chimney. The body was identified as James S.-H., a well-known burglar, from a set of dentures made while he was in prison ten years before.

❋

An escaping burglar who slashed his leg as he leapt through a window asked the householder to call an ambulance as he lay bleeding on the lawn. He died in the hospital.

❋

A bank robber in Sydney was killed by a security screen that sprang up from the counter and pinned him against the ceiling. The man, who had earlier jumped on the counter and threatened the staff with a machete, was crushed to death.

Allan McQ., of Kansas City, died on a Los Angeles–bound flight from Lima when plastic packets of cocaine he was smuggling in his stomach burst open, Peruvian police said.

THE BEST LAID PLANS

Hunting rabbits

A man hunting rabbits was found wedged headfirst up to his waist in a warren. Paul F. had set out from his home at 7:00 A.M. with his ferret and six terriers. The ferret or one of the terriers is thought to have become stuck down the hole, which Mr. F. widened in his efforts to reach the animal.

Juan C., a gamekeeper, was in jail in the southern Spanish city of Granada after shooting what he thought was an eagle in a bush. The bird turned out to be Adrian M., who fell from the bush dead.

The imitation duck calls made by Dimitris T. when he went out shooting in Salonika were so lifelike that two of his colleagues fired at the bushes where he was hiding and shot him dead.

A Kenyan Masai warrior threw his spear at a shadow he thought was a lion threatening his flocks, to find that he had killed his wife.

❋

David D. accidentally shot his friend dead while attempting to cure his hiccups by scaring him with a gun.

❋

An amateur actor was shot dead on the stage in Rouen by an actress during a scene from a Wild West play. René D. was shot in the back by a gun meant to contain only blanks.

※

An eighteen-year-old French paratrooper who committed suicide during rifle practice at Millau inadvertently killed another soldier as well. The bullet fired by Pascal Th. passed through his body and hit Charles M., standing thirty yards away.

※

Mrs. Nancy S. killed her husband, son, and daughter when she committed suicide in her car in their Holly-wood, Florida, garage. The air-conditioning system in the house circulated the carbon monoxide from the garage, killing the entire family.

※

A twenty-four-year-old man became so excited, possibly after deciding to kill himself, that his heart stopped beating, an inquest at Northampton was told. The emotional state of his heart, coupled with a rush of adrenaline, could have caused Mr. Stephen B. to die of natural causes.

※

A twenty-nine-year-old security guard, Sergio L., shot himself dead while demonstrating to friends the Russian roulette scenes from the film *The Deer Hunter,* Milan police said.

Farmer Mark G. died in a blazing cornfield at Hadleigh, Suffolk, after he set out alone to burn off stubble.

❇

The perils of carrying extra gasoline in a car were illustrated by the case of the motorist who died after driving off the road and into a ditch. He had fitted his vehicle with an extra twenty-gallon gas tank and had three full cans in the trunk. Some of the fuel spilled out. The police reported: "As the operator spun the tires, trying to get out of the ditch, the gas ignited and the car became engulfed in flames."

❇

A man who used a cigarette lighter to search for a friend caused a fire that killed the friend, engulfed two huge oil storage tanks, and forced the evacuation of most inhabitants of Gilbertown, Alabama.

❋

A music student died after being caught in a flash fire while apparently trying to relieve his piles. Norik H., of Kensington, was found naked. The fumes from an open bottle of gasoline had been ignited by a hotplate. His brother Hiak said relieving piles with paraffin was an old family remedy, but it was possible Norik had used gasoline.

❋

A chain saw that jammed caused the death of Mr. Gordon P., a tree-feller of Northamptonshire. Miss Jane

G. said that she had twice warned Mr. P. about the danger of the tree, a fifty-one-foot diseased elm, falling the wrong way. "But the saw jammed and he was determined to get it out," she said. He began running as the tree fell, but he slipped and the tree fell on him.

※

Mr. Donald D. died when a huge hollow oak he was helping to fell caught fire and crashed down on him. A policeman said that when fire broke out in the hollow of the tree, Mr. D. went to investigate and could not get out of the way in time when the tree crashed.

※

OUT & ABOUT

Automatic doors

A fifty-two-year-old Frenchman was killed when the automatic doors of a train closed on his neck in a Paris suburb, police said.

❋

A man was hanged from a window while trying to break into his own house. John W. was trapped and caught by his clothing when his makeshift ladder of a chest of drawers and plant pots collapsed.

❋

A cocked pistol stuck in the belt of Señor Gonzalo M., mayor of Candaba, Philippines, shot him dead when he slammed his car door on it.

❋

A snake shot a hunter dead after coiling around the trigger of his shotgun. Ali A. tried to catch the snake alive by pressing the butt of his shotgun against its head. But the snake coiled itself around the butt and hit the trigger with its thrashing tail, firing one of the barrels and shooting Ali in the head.

❋

During a particularly heavy storm, a farmer at Vastres, near St.-Etienne, was sucked out of the window and impaled on the fence of his chicken run.

❋

Patrick M. was killed in the garden of his home in Birmingham when an empty aluminum beer cask exploded on a bonfire. A section of the nine-gallon barrel flew over the rooftops and smashed a church window one hundred yards away.

❄

A trainee chef died with his neck trapped in the electric window of his Fiat. A coroner left open the question of blame in the case.

❄

The body of Monsieur André D., a wine producer, was found in a vat of fermenting grapes. He apparently had been asphyxiated by the fumes.

❄

GRAVE
REPORTS

The Sighthill shortcut

Edward McG., of Glasgow, was killed when a tombstone fell on him while he and two companions were taking a short cut through Sighthill Cemetery, Glasgow.

※

Sixty-three-year-old widow Mrs. Carmella T., of Sicily, is believed to have died from a heart attack after being stung by wasps while arranging flowers beside her sister's grave at a cemetery in Southend-on-Sea, Essex.

※

A South Korean who, upon the advice of a geomancer, tried to turn around a run of bad luck by moving his father's tomb, collapsed and died after opening the coffin and discovering his father's body had not decomposed fifteen years after he was buried.

Five people leapt to their deaths off a fast-moving truck, panic-stricken by the sight of a man emerging from a coffin that lay beside them on the vehicle's back, officials in Bujumbura, Burundi, said. The five had hitched a ride with the driver, who had bought the coffin to bury a relative. But before the passengers got on, his co-driver had slipped into the coffin to take a nap. He closed the coffin to keep out the rain and never realized that hitchhikers had been picked up. When he woke up and removed the lid, the scared passengers jumped off.